D1406155

SEE-THROUGH
REPTILES

STEVE PARKER
ILLUSTRATED BY ROD FERRING

RUNNING PRESS
KIDS

CONTENTS

Text © 2004 The Ilex Press Limited
First published in the United States in 2004
by Running Press Kids, an imprint of
Running Press Book Publishers.
All rights reserved under the Pan-American
and International Copyright Conventions.
Printed in China.

This book may not be reproduced in whole
or in part, in any form or by any means,
electronic or mechanical, including
photocopying, recording, or by any
information storage and retrieval system now
known or hereafter invented, without written
permission from the publisher.

9 8 7 6 5 4 3 2 1
Digit on the right indicates the number
of this printing

Library of Congress
Control Number: 2004091780

ISBN 0-7624-1989-X

This book was created by
THE ILEX PRESS LTD
Cambridge CB2 4LX

PUBLISHER Alastair Campbell
EXECUTIVE PUBLISHER Sophie Collins
CREATIVE DIRECTOR Peter Bridgewater
EDITORIAL DIRECTOR Steve Luck
DESIGN MANAGER Tony Seddon
SENIOR PROJECT EDITOR Caroline Earle
DESIGNER Wayne Blades
ILLUSTRATOR Rod Ferring

This book may be ordered by mail from the
publisher. Please include $2.50 for postage and
handling. But try your bookstore first!

Running Press Book Publishers
125 South Twenty-second Street
Philadelphia, Pennsylvania 19103-4399

Visit us on the web!
www.runningpress.com

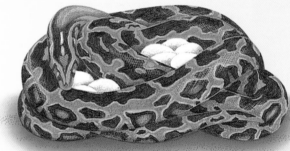

REPTILES PAST AND PRESENT

What is a reptile? Is it a cold, scaly, creepy-crawly creature with long legs and a bendable tail, which hunts mice at night and breeds by laying eggs? Partly, yes—lizards are reptiles, and some fit this description. But many reptiles do not. Other lizards have hardly any scales and are warm to the touch. Snakes have no legs. Some tortoises have no tails. Crocodiles hunt by day for prey much bigger than mice. And some snakes do not lay eggs but have live babies! But all reptiles have one feature in common. This is a skeleton of bones inside the body, with a backbone (spinal column) along the middle. So reptiles are backboned animals, or vertebrates, along with fish, frogs and other amphibians, birds, and mammals like ourselves.

THE FIRST REPTILE?

Reptiles have been on Earth far longer than people—hundreds of millions of years. Scientists have found their remains buried in rocks, as fossils of their bones that have turned to stone. One of the earliest reptiles was *Hylonomus*, from the Carboniferous Period about 300 million years ago. It was small and slim—its head and body were hardly larger than a human finger. It looked like a lizard, but the lizard group of reptiles did not begin until millions of years later. About 50 million years later, reptiles had spread around the world and were very common.

HYLONOMUS

OUR DISTANT ANCESTORS?

We belong to the animal group called mammals, which are furry and warm-blooded. The first small, shrewlike mammals darted away from the feet of early dinosaurs, over 200 million years ago. They had probably evolved from reptiles called therapsids, which gradually grew fur instead of scales, became warm-blooded, and bred by giving birth to babies rather than laying eggs.

▷ *Thrinaxodon*
Thrinaxodon was a reptile—but only just, because it was nearly a mammal, too. It had many mammal features like fur, teeth of different shapes, and tiny bones inside its ears. About the size of a pet cat, it lived 220 million years ago in what is now Southern Africa.

THRINAXODON

THE AGE OF REPTILES

The time known as the Mesozoic Era, from 250 to 65 million years ago, saw reptiles as the main large animals on land, in the sea, and in the air. Hundreds of kinds of dinosaurs thundered and raced over the ground, while *pterosaurs* flapped high above. Under the waves lurked fierce, fast-swimming reptiles like the dolphin-shaped *ichthyosaurs*, round-bodied *plesiosaurs*, and huge-fanged *pliosaurs* and *mosasaurs*.

▷ **End of an era**
Mesozoic reptiles ruled the land, air, and sea. But 65 million years ago a great disaster wiped out dinosaurs, *pterosaurs*, and other kinds of reptiles. Only some types, like turtles, survived.

FEATHERY DINOSAURS?

Today, only birds have feathers. But fossils show that some dinosaurs had feathers, too! Most scientists believe that the first birds appeared by change, or evolution, from small meat-eating dinosaurs. Their scales changed into feathers, their front legs became wings, and they learned to flap and fly.

▷ *Archaeopteryx*
One of the first birds was *Archaeopteryx*. It lived 150 million years ago in regions that are now Germany and France. About the size of a chicken, *Archaeopteryx* had feathers and wings. But it also had a long, bony tail and teeth in its beak—unlike any bird today.

PTEROSAURS

TYRANNOSAURUS

PREHISTORIC TURTLE

TRICERATOPS

THE RANGE OF REPTILES

There are nearly 8,000 different kinds or species of reptiles living almost all over the world. Reptiles have spread to nearly every type of surrounding or habitat, from high hills and thick forests to grasslands, deserts, swamps, rivers, lakes, seashores, and the wide-open ocean. The only places that lack reptiles are the coldest mountain-tops and polar regions, and the deep sea. Scientists divide reptiles into about six main groups, depending on the features inside their bodies, especially the shapes of the bones. These groups are lizards, snakes, turtles and tortoises, crocodiles and alligators, and the lesser-known amphisbaenians and tuataras.

NOT WORMS, NOT LIZARDS

Amphisbaenians are curious reptiles that lack legs, and are sometimes called "worm-lizards." They are not lizards, nor worms, although they are worm-shaped and burrow in the soil. There are about 160 species and they live mainly in the damp soil of tropical forests. They are all fierce hunters of prey such as grubs, slugs, insects, and real worms.

△ **Florida worm-lizard**
The Florida worm-lizard is about 8 inches (20 cm) long and is as slim as a pencil. It pushes through the earth with its shovel-shaped head as it hunts worms, bugs, and other small soil creatures.

"LEFTOVER" FROM ANCIENT TIMES

The tuatara looks like a lizard, but is not. This very strange creature is the only survivor from an ancient group of reptiles that thrived during the Age of Dinosaurs, 200 million years ago. There are only two species of tuatara, and they are found only on small islands off the New Zealand coast. They rest in burrows by day and emerge after dusk to hunt insects, spiders, slugs, and worms.

△ **Tuatara**
The tuatara is about 24 inches (60 cm) from nose to tail. It is thought to live to a great age, perhaps over 100 years. It also breeds very slowly—its eggs take more than one year to hatch. But it is extremely rare and the few remaining tuataras, and their island habitats, need careful conservation.

BY FAR THE BIGGEST GROUP

Lizards are by far the largest group of reptiles, with more than 4,500 species—more than half the number in the entire reptile group. Most have a long and slim body, legs, and tail, and are active predators. Some are omnivores, eating both animals and plants, while a few are herbivores and consume only plant foods.

REPTILE ROUND-UP

Life on the ocean wave

- Some snakes live their entire lives in the sea. There are about 50 kinds of sea snakes, which are members of the cobra group.
- Most sea snakes are found in the warm waters of the Indian and Pacific Oceans.
- Sea snakes have very powerful poison and bite prey such as fish.
- Most kinds never come to land. They even breed at sea, giving birth to baby snakes rather than laying eggs.
- Out of water, sea snakes can hardly move—their muscles are too floppy.

△ **Most widespread snake**
The yellow-bellied or pelagic sea snake is the world's most widespread snake, found across the vast Pacific and Indian Oceans. It grows to about 3 feet (1 meter) long, eats small fish, and swims by swishing its black-blotched, oarlike tail.

◁ **Reptile claws**
Apart from snakes and amphisbaenians, almost all reptiles have claws on their toes. Some lizards have very long and sharp claws, like the ones on this green tree monitor (*left*). This shows that they are good climbers, using their claws to grip into the bark of trees.

BIGGEST AND FIERCEST

The biggest reptiles are crocodiles, alligators, and caimans, known as the crocodilians. But they form one of the smallest reptile groups, with only 23 species. Like most reptiles, they are meat-eaters, or carnivores. Most live in and around water in rivers, lakes, marshes, and swamps in the warmer parts of the world.

◁ **Chinese alligator**
The Chinese alligator is one of the smallest crocodilians, less than 7 feet (2 meters) in length. It is rare and lives only in the region of the Chang Jiang (Yangtze) River in China. Like many reptiles, it is inactive in cold weather and "sleeps" in a cave or buried in the mud. Many reptiles hardly move in cold weather. This inactivity is known as torpor.

SLITHERING ALONG

There are more than 2,900 different species of snakes. They are closely related to lizards and are included with them in the reptile "supergroup" called the squamates. Most reptiles have bodies covered with scales, which are especially clear in snakes. All snakes swallow their prey whole.

Scales overlap like tiles on a roof.

Front edge of scale is fixed into skin.

Rear edge of scale can be lifted above skin.

ALL-AROUND SHELL

Three hundred species, including turtles, terrapins, and tortoises all form the reptile group known as chelonians. They are unmistakable with their hard wraparound shells for protection. Because they are heavy and slow, they cannot race after prey. So most wait in hiding to ambush victims or feed on varied foods, including small creatures, fruits, leaves, and other plant matter.

▽ **Snake-necked turtle**
The snake-necked turtle of Australia has a snakelike head and neck on a shelled body. In rivers and lakes, it darts its head to and fro to snap at fish and other prey swimming past.

△ **Belly scales**
The belly scales of large snakes like the emerald tree boa are very big. The snake tilts them slightly so it can push their sharp edges against the ground, to slide along.

CROCS AND 'GATORS

An old log floats slowly along a north Australian river as kangaroos, cattle, and other animals come to drink. The "log" quietly slips under the surface, and suddenly there is a massive splash as a crocodile lunges up from the water near the bank and grabs a victim. After a huge struggle, the croc drags its prey under the water where it drowns. Then the crocodile can clamp its powerful jaws onto the body and spin around like a top, to tear off a leg for swallowing. Most crocodiles, alligators, and caimans hunt like this—they are ambush predators, colored in drab greens and browns for camouflage.

DESIGNED FOR AMBUSH

All crocodilians have the same basic body plan. The jaws are large and long, studded with many conical teeth. The eyes and the nostrils at the nose-tip are set high on the head, so the croc can float almost hidden under the surface but still see, breathe, and smell. The tail is long and high-ridged, and swishes from side to side for powerful swimming. A croc usually walks slowly, its legs sprawled out sideways, but it can also raise its body high and "gallop" as fast as you can run!

BIGGEST LIVING REPTILE

The saltwater, or estuarine, crocodile is the largest reptile in the world (although not as long as some snakes). It can grow to 23 feet (7 meters) in length and weigh one ton. It is also called the Indo-Pacific crocodile because it is found along the coasts and rivers of the eastern Indian and western Pacific Oceans. As its name suggests, it is one of the few crocodiles at home in the sea as well as fresh water.

△ A fierce "smile"
Teeth are one of the differences between crocodiles and alligators. In 'gators, the teeth are mostly hidden when the mouth is closed. In crocs, the fourth tooth from the front in the lower jaw fits into a notch in the upper jaw, and can be seen from the outside.

△ Powerful swimmer
The saltwater crocodile has been seen swimming strongly many miles from shore. But it also travels up rivers and into lakes. It has attacked many humans over the years, especially in northern Australia and the countries of Southeast Asia.

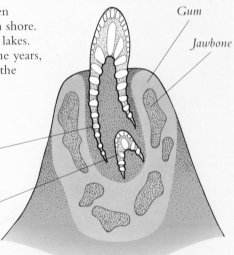

Gum

Jawbone

Each tooth is shaped like a tall cone with a blunt tip.

New tooth pushing older tooth out.

◁ Nile crocodile
The Nile crocodile of Africa attacks many more people each year than do big cats like lions and leopards. It grows to 16 feet (5 meters) long and eats whatever it can catch, from fish and waterbirds to full-grown zebra, wildebeest, and even the fearsome, huge-horned, half-ton African buffalo.

△ Croc teeth
A typical croc has 50–60 teeth. Each tooth lasts about one year and then falls out, but is quickly replaced by another tooth growing up from the jawbone and gum. This happens with different teeth at different times, so a croc always has some small young teeth and some large older teeth in its mouth.

RARE TO COMMON

The gharial (or gavial) was once rare. But gharials have been captured and bred in fenced-in ponds, and then released into the wild, to increase their numbers in natural habitats. The gharial is one of the longest crocodiles, at 23 feet (7 meters), but fairly slim. Its legs are small but its wide webbed feet show that it swims very well.

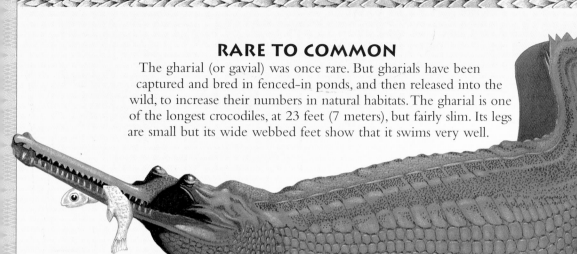

REPTILE ROUND-UP

Who lives where?

• The five species of caimans all live in South and Central America.
• The Nile crocodile lives in most parts of Africa.
• The slender-snouted and dwarf crocodiles also live in Africa.
• There are only two kinds of alligator. These are the Chinese alligator (*see page 5*), and the American alligator in the far southeast of North America.
• The American, Cuban, Orinoco, and Morelet's crocodiles also live in warmer parts of the Americas.

△ **Male gharial**
The male gharial has a lump, or "pot," on its nose, which the female lacks. The very long, slender mouth can swish speedily through the water in a sideways swipe, to catch fish, the gharial's main food. Gharials are found in southern Asia, especially India.

COOL CAIMAN

Caimans are close cousins of alligators and live mainly in South America. They have blunter, more rounded snouts than crocodiles and live mainly in swampy areas, such as along the Amazon River. They eat mostly fish, but the bigger types prey on mammals such as the piglike tapirs.

△ **Black caiman**
The black caiman, at almost 20 feet (6 meters) long, is the biggest predator in South America. Like many reptiles, it opens or "gapes" its mouth if it gets too hot, like a panting dog, to lose heat from the inner lining.

DANGEROUS WATERS

The mugger is a wide-set, powerful crocodile from India. It lives in all kinds of fresh waters, including irrigation ditches and reservoirs that store water for farm animals. There are several attacks each year on people, as farm workers clear out ditches or take their animals to drink.

▽ **Mugger**
The mugger reaches lengths of more than 13 feet (4 meters), and is very low-set and heavily built. In some regions of India, it has learned to take fish from nets—it rips the nets and endangers the people in their small boats.

GOOD MOTHER 'GATOR

People once thought that crocodiles and alligators ate their babies because these great reptiles were seen with young in their mouths. Now we know that they are really looking after their offspring. Like most reptiles, crocs and alligators breed by laying eggs. Reptile mothers generally lay the eggs and then leave. They do not guard the eggs or look after their young. But crocodiles and alligators, like this American alligator, are much more caring parents.

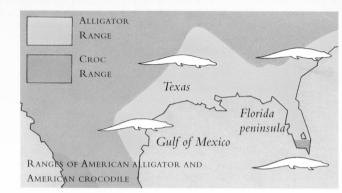

ALLIGATOR RANGE

CROC RANGE

Texas

Florida peninsula

Gulf of Mexico

RANGES OF AMERICAN ALLIGATOR AND AMERICAN CROCODILE

◁ **Wide-ranging 'gators**
American alligators have increased their range in the past 20 years, especially in Texas, where they live in pools and canals made to hold water that cattle drink.

Tiny embryo

Layers of yolk

Paperlike membrane lining shell

△ **'Gator egg**
Each egg is about 2–3 inches (6–8 cm) long, with a creamy white, fairly hard shell. Inside the egg, the baby alligator starts off as a tiny speck, small as a pinhead.

THE ALLIGATOR'S HOME

American alligators live wild in the southeastern USA, especially in Florida and Louisiana. Their cousin, the American crocodile, also lives in southern Florida. The young alligators grow faster in the warmer south, and slower farther north where the climate is cooler. They start to breed when they reach a length of about 6 feet (190 cm).

BREEDING TIME

It's alligator breeding time in southeast North America. In April and May, the males roar to attract females. The partners get together in the water and bump, nudge, and press each other. After mating, the female begins to prepare her nest. The male wanders off—he takes no part in baby care.

GIRL OR BOY?

Inside the egg, the young alligator grows from a tiny speck to a fully formed baby. Whether it's a female or male depends largely on the temperature of the nest mound. If it's less than 88°F (31°C), most babies will be females. If the mound is more than 90°F (32°C), most will be male. In between, 88–90°F (31–32°C), the babies are a mixture of females and males.

The mother 'gator selects a shady area near the water to build the nest.

The mother 'gator uses her back feet to dig a hole.

△ **Preparing the nest**
The female alligator scratches and pulls together leaves, twigs, and other bits of plants, to make a large pile.

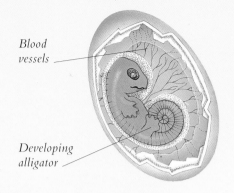

Blood vessels

Developing alligator

△ Nutritious yolk
The baby feeds on a store of nutrients in the form of yellow yolk (like a hen's egg), which are carried to the developing 'gator along tiny blood vessels.

LAYING THE EGGS
The mother alligator presses and squashes her nest pile into a smooth mound about 20–28 inches (50–70 cm) high and 6 feet (180 cm) across. Then she scoops away a hole at the top with her back feet, to lay her eggs. The eggs emerge about one every half-minute. When they are all laid, the mother covers over the hole so the eggs are safe inside the mound.

The babies start to squeak when they are ready to hatch.

▷ 'Gators galore
A young mother alligator, 10–15 years old, lays about 30 eggs. When she is older, she may lay 50 or more.

SQUEAK, GRUNT
The alligator's nest mound is like a compost heap in the garden— the rotting plants make it warm. The babies develop inside their eggs and are ready to hatch in about nine weeks. Then they grunt and squeak to tell their mother. She may help them by digging the eggs out of the mound and gently cracking the shells in her massive mouth.

▷ Carried to safety
After the baby 'gators hatch, their mother carries them to a safe pool in her mouth, and guards them for several months.

▽ Ready to hatch
When the baby alligator reaches about 9 inches (25 cm) long and 2 ounces (50 grams) in weight, it is ready to hatch.

The baby alligator bites its way out of the shell using a special "egg tooth."

REPTILE ROUND-UP

How fast do they grow?

- Reptiles' rate of growth varies from one individual to the next. The more they eat, and the warmer their surroundings, the faster they grow.
- In most reptiles, growth continues all through life. But its rate slows down greatly with increasing age.
- By 5 years, most American alligators are about 4 feet (120 cm) long.
- By 25 years, males are about 10 feet (3 meters) and females are closer to 8 feet (2.5 meters).
- By 50 years old, males are 13 feet (4 meters) and females almost 10 feet (3 meters).

LIZARDS GALORE!

Lizards are the most common and widespread of all reptiles. They are also the most varied. The smallest could sit on your little finger, while the biggest are longer than a car. Some lizards have tails twice as long as their bodies, while others have no tail. Some have long spindly legs, yet others have no legs at all and look more like snakes. Some lizards are wide and tubby, while others are thinner than pencils. Different lizards dwell in almost every habitat on land, and there are many who live in fresh water, too, but only one kind lives in the sea.

THE DANGEROUS DRAGON

The biggest of all lizards is the Komodo dragon. It lives on a few islands in Indonesia, Southeast Asia. It is a powerful predator with big claws and teeth, muscular legs and body, and a tail that makes up half its total length. It grabs victims in its wide, sharp-toothed jaws and tears them to pieces, or bites them hard so they bleed to death. But these "dragons" are rare, with fewer than 5,000 left.

LIVING FLYPAPER

Geckos are mostly small, common lizards of tropical places. They are active at night and named after the sharp, barklike call that they make, especially in the breeding season. There are almost 700 kinds and some are familiar in houses, where they are helpful in catching flies, mosquitoes, spiders, and other pests. A gecko's feet are covered with thousands of tiny brushlike pads, which grip so well that it can run up walls and windows, and even hang from the ceiling.

△ **House gecko**
The common house gecko of India and Southeast Asia is about as long as a human hand. If it is attacked, it squeaks loudly and also sheds its tail to distract its enemy. The tail comes away at a special place, without much harm to the gecko, and soon grows again.

▽ **Komodo dragon**
At 10 feet (3 meters) long, and weighing more than 220 pounds (100 kg), few animals can escape the Komodo dragon. This giant lizard can eat half of its own weight at one meal, such as a goat, deer—and, rarely, a human being.

◁ **Flying lizard**
The flying lizard is about 8 inches (20 cm) long. It is an expert climber and its favorite foods are tree ants. But it is hunted by snakes and birds such as forest hawks.

SWOOPING AROUND

The flying lizard of Southeast Asia has "wings" of skin on the extra-long rib bones of its chest. It cannot really fly, but it glides well. Usually it lives in trees and swoops from one to another, to find food or escape predators. Its wings are folded along its sides when not gliding.

FRIGHTENING FRILL

The frilled lizard of Australia has an amazing way to frighten enemies. It stands up on its back legs, sways from side to side, opens its mouth wide, hisses loudly, and makes a large, bright frill of skin stand out around its head. The frill is held out by thin rods of gristle and usually lies flat along its shoulders.

LAND OF LIZARDS

Australia is mostly dry grassland and desert—and reptiles thrive there. There are more than 400 kinds of skinks, monitors, and other lizards, including the second-biggest type in the world, the perentie. It is strong enough to catch young kangaroos and small wallabies.

△ **Frilled lizard**
The frilled lizard is a type of iguana. It grows to 24 inches (60 cm) long and feeds mainly on small ground animals like insects, spiders, grubs, and occasionally mice.

SWIMMING IN SAND

There are nearly 2,000 kinds of skinks—the largest lizard group. Most are small, slim, and fast-moving, with short legs. Sand skinks have such tiny legs, they are almost useless. The sand skink lives in soft sand and "swims" along by wriggling through the loose grains. Many other lizards that live in sand or soil also have tiny legs, or even none at all.

△ **Sand skink**
The sand skink's mini-legs have just one toe each on the front legs and two toes at the rear. This super-slim lizard is only 5 inches (12 cm) long and eats termites and small grubs.

SUNBATHING AT THE SEASIDE

The only lizard that swims regularly in the sea is the Galapagos marine iguana. It lives around the shores of the Galapagos Islands in the eastern Pacific Ocean. It can dive down to 33 feet (10 meters) to reach its main food of soft seaweeds. After a dive in the cool water, this lizard sunbathes on rocks to warm its body.

▷ **Perentie**
The perentie reaches 8 feet (2.5 meters) in length, and fears few other animals. It has a bright pattern of spots and patches in shades of cream, yellow, and brown. This gives perfect camouflage among the dry sands, rocks, and grasses of central Australia.

▷ **Galapagos marine iguana**
At 3 feet (1 meter) long, the Galapagos marine iguana is a large and strong lizard. It has the ability to stay underwater for more than a half-hour, although its usual feeding dives last just a few minutes.

NOW YOU SEE ME...

The chameleon is a very strange lizard. It creeps through the branches, holding on strongly with its pincerlike toes and curly tail. Its body is tall and long, but almost as thin as a leaf. What's more, the chameleon can change color to match the leaves and twigs around it. And usually, it sneaks along so slowly that it is hardly noticed. Yet this lizard can also make movements too fast for us to see. One moment there's an insect near the chameleon, then in a flash—it's gone!

TWO VIEWS

The chameleon's beady eyes are on top of cone-shaped, moveable "turrets." Each eye can turn or swivel to look in a different direction. So the chameleon can see to the front and back at the same time, or both up and down. Can you?

READY TO STRIKE

As the chameleon creeps from tree to tree, it adjusts its body color to match the shade of the leaves there. Then it settles down to wait. Eventually a small creature like an insect or spider comes near. The chameleon's amazing eyes swivel around to get a good view. Its legs shift very slightly, and it leans slowly toward the victim...

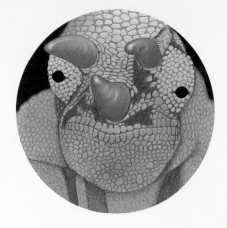

△ **Swivel eyes**
This Jackson's chameleon is looking to the front, and out to the side, too! Its mouth has many tiny teeth along the edges of the jaws.

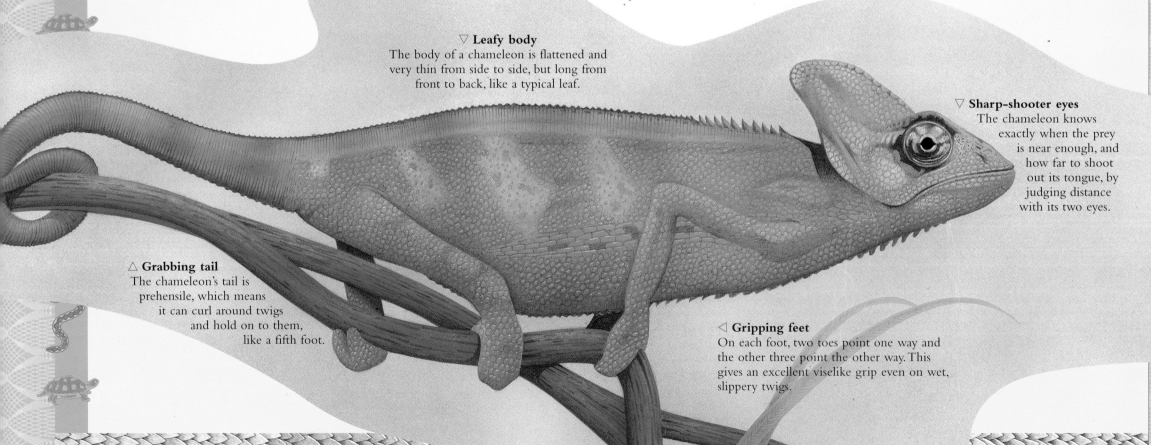

▽ **Leafy body**
The body of a chameleon is flattened and very thin from side to side, but long from front to back, like a typical leaf.

▽ **Sharp-shooter eyes**
The chameleon knows exactly when the prey is near enough, and how far to shoot out its tongue, by judging distance with its two eyes.

△ **Grabbing tail**
The chameleon's tail is prehensile, which means it can curl around twigs and hold on to them, like a fifth foot.

◁ **Gripping feet**
On each foot, two toes point one way and the other three point the other way. This gives an excellent viselike grip even on wet, slippery twigs.

CHAMELEON KALEIDOSCOPE

Chameleons are famous for changing color. But this is more complicated than it seems. Sometimes a chameleon alters its color and pattern as camouflage, to match the surroundings. But there are other reasons for changing color, such as the chameleon being relaxed, or angry, or frightened. If one chameleon sees another of its kind nearby, it may become darker with stripes, or lighter and brighter. This depends on whether the chameleon is trying to frighten away the intruder into its home territory—or is inviting it in as a mate!

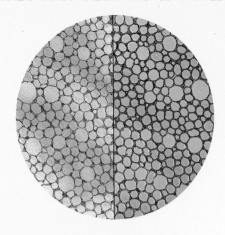

△ **Green to brown**
When waiting for prey, the chameleon matches the leaves around it. A frightened chameleon turns dark brown or almost black, perhaps with yellow or white spots. At night when resting, a chameleon may become very pale yellow or green, or even creamy-white.

A BIG FAMILY

There are more than 90 kinds of chameleons. About half of these live on the island of Madagascar, east of Africa. Most of the others are found across Africa, with a few in South Asia and one species in Europe.

▷ **Chameleon collection**
The Namaqua chameleon is about 6 inches (15 cm) long. It lives among the rocks and sands of dry Southern Africa, and even in the scorching Namib Desert. The flap-necked chameleon can lift the flaps of skin over its neck to look bigger and fiercer. The male Jackson's chameleon has three long horns on his head. The female has only one very small nose horn. Parson's chameleon is one of the biggest, growing to more than 24 inches (60 cm) long, including its tail.

NAMAQUA CHAMELEON

FLAP-NECKED CHAMELEON

JACKSON'S CHAMELEON

PARSONS' CHAMELEON

▽ **Spring-back tongue**
The tongue will flick back like a rubber band, then the chameleon closes its mouth to squash and swallow its meal.

LONG, LONG TONGUE

...Then FLICK! The chameleon shoots out its incredible tongue—which can be as long as its whole head and body! The tongue is normally squashed shorter into the large mouth, like an elastic band that is not stretched. As it shoots out, it becomes long and narrow, and grabs the prey on its sticky tip. The tip also bends like a suction cup to squelch onto the insect. The whole process takes 1/20 of a second—faster than you can blink.

◁ **Slimy-suckered tip**
The blob-shaped end of the tongue has a sticky, slimy covering that grabs and holds the victim.

▷ **Cha-meal-eon meals**
Most chameleons eat any kind of insect, spider, bug, or creepy-crawly that they can catch. They ignore the stings of wasps, bees and ants, the hard body-casings of beetles, the sharp fangs of centipedes and spiders, and the spiky kicking legs of grasshoppers and crickets—and gulp down the lot!

△ **Brookesia chameleon**
Most chameleons live in woods and forests. The smallest kinds, like brookesias, are hardly larger than your finger! The tree brookesia of central Africa has ridges on its sides. These resemble the stripes or veins of a leaf, making its small body even better camouflaged. Its cousin the brown brookesia is even tinier, just 3 inches (8 cm) from nose to tail-tip. It lives on the ground and cannot change color very well, staying mainly brown. But this hides it perfectly among the dead leaves on the forest floor.

BEWARE THE SNAKE!

Snakes have no legs. Yet they can move extremely well. Most kinds are able to slither fast over the ground, burrow in loose soil, swim well, climb trees rapidly, and a few kinds can even fly—or at least, glide. Snakes are the ultimate predators—nearly all catch their own victims and swallow them whole, alive or dead. They are often feared as being deadly to people, but only about 50 of the 2,900 species are truly dangerous to humans. Most of these have poisonous bites, while a few can coil around a person-sized victim and squeeze it to death.

SILENT SWIMMER

Many snakes are at home in water. They dive in to get away from predators and also swim slowly and silently with hardly a ripple as they look for prey. The grass snake often hunts in ponds, ditches, and lakes for victims such as fish, frogs, and baby waterbirds.

◁ **Grass snake**

The grass snake could easily be called the marsh snake, since it is very common around marshy pools and swampy bogs. It is widespread across Europe and Asia, and grows to nearly 7 feet (2 meters) long.

SPIT IN THE EYE

Poisonous snakes stab their venom into the victims as they bite. But the spitting cobra has another use for its venom. The poison is squirted through small holes in its fangs, as a spray that can travel more than 7 feet (2 meters). The cobra "spits" to defend itself against enemies.

◁ **Spitting cobra**

The poison liquid of the cobra's "spit" does not usually kill an enemy. But it causes pain on sensitive skin, and if it lands in the eyes, it can lead to blindness.

◁ **Vine snake**

The amazing vine snake of South America is up to 7 feet (2 meters) long, but as thin as a finger. It drapes itself over tree branches like a creeper or vine, waiting for baby birds or young lizards to come within biting range.

CAN YOU SEE ME?

Some snakes race after their prey. But many lie in wait for victims to come near. These ambush predators are usually camouflaged by color and shape to blend into their surroundings. Those with patches of brown, yellow, and green often lie on the forest floor, while those with brown and yellow stripes live in grasslands, and mainly green snakes are found among leaves in trees.

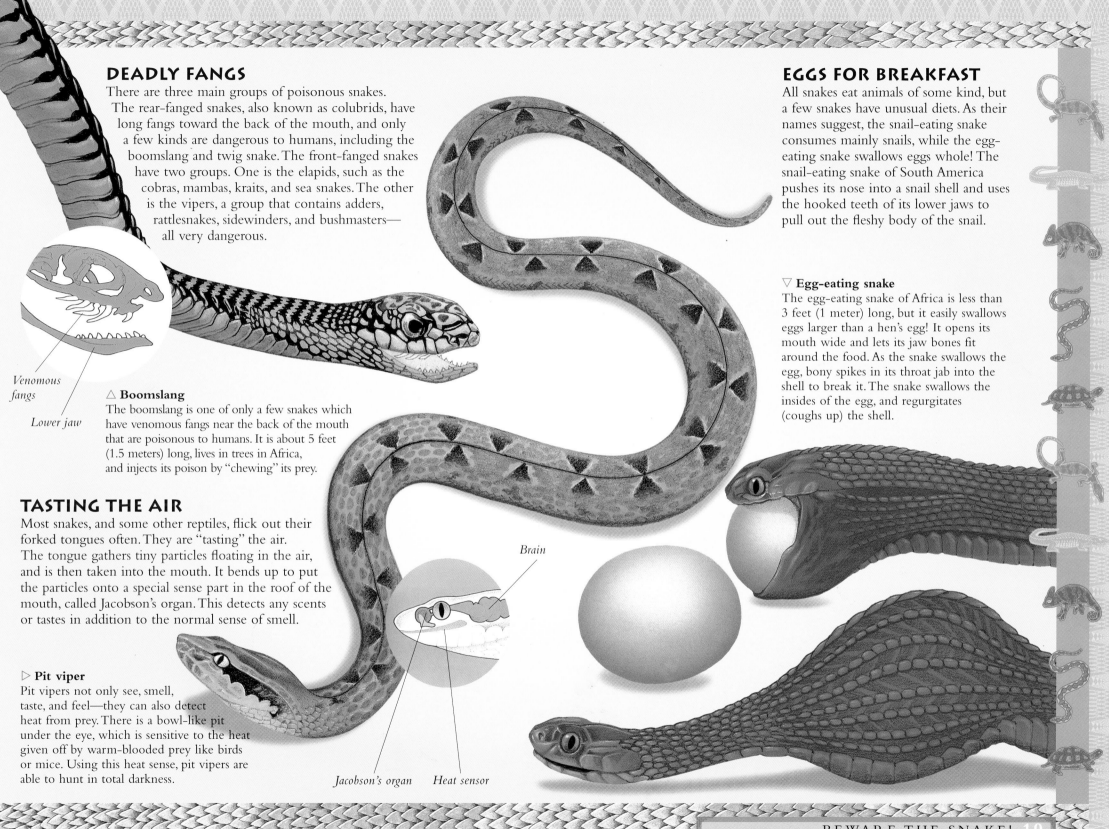

DEADLY FANGS

There are three main groups of poisonous snakes. The rear-fanged snakes, also known as colubrids, have long fangs toward the back of the mouth, and only a few kinds are dangerous to humans, including the boomslang and twig snake. The front-fanged snakes have two groups. One is the elapids, such as the cobras, mambas, kraits, and sea snakes. The other is the vipers, a group that contains adders, rattlesnakes, sidewinders, and bushmasters—all very dangerous.

Venomous fangs

Lower jaw

△ **Boomslang**
The boomslang is one of only a few snakes which have venomous fangs near the back of the mouth that are poisonous to humans. It is about 5 feet (1.5 meters) long, lives in trees in Africa, and injects its poison by "chewing" its prey.

TASTING THE AIR

Most snakes, and some other reptiles, flick out their forked tongues often. They are "tasting" the air. The tongue gathers tiny particles floating in the air, and is then taken into the mouth. It bends up to put the particles onto a special sense part in the roof of the mouth, called Jacobson's organ. This detects any scents or tastes in addition to the normal sense of smell.

▷ **Pit viper**
Pit vipers not only see, smell, taste, and feel—they can also detect heat from prey. There is a bowl-like pit under the eye, which is sensitive to the heat given off by warm-blooded prey like birds or mice. Using this heat sense, pit vipers are able to hunt in total darkness.

Jacobson's organ   *Heat sensor*

Brain

EGGS FOR BREAKFAST

All snakes eat animals of some kind, but a few snakes have unusual diets. As their names suggest, the snail-eating snake consumes mainly snails, while the egg-eating snake swallows eggs whole! The snail-eating snake of South America pushes its nose into a snail shell and uses the hooked teeth of its lower jaws to pull out the fleshy body of the snail.

▽ **Egg-eating snake**
The egg-eating snake of Africa is less than 3 feet (1 meter) long, but it easily swallows eggs larger than a hen's egg! It opens its mouth wide and lets its jaw bones fit around the food. As the snake swallows the egg, bony spikes in its throat jab into the shell to break it. The snake swallows the insides of the egg, and regurgitates (coughs up) the shell.

A MASSIVE MOUTHFUL

All snakes eat their prey alive, or perhaps just freshly killed. And often the prey is big—it may be much wider than the snake itself. But this is not a worry. Snakes have very stretchy mouths and bendy jaws with hinged bones. A snake can open its mouth wider and wider, like a rubber tube, to wriggle itself over the meal. Can you imagine eating all your meals for the next three months in one giant mouthful?

THE BITE OF DEATH

Most poisonous snakes, like rattlesnakes, vipers, and adders, have long teeth called fangs at the upper front of the mouth. These lie folded back against the upper jaw when not in use. As the snake opens its mouth and strikes, the fangs swing down to stab quickly into the victim. The snake then backs off, and watches and waits for the poison to work.

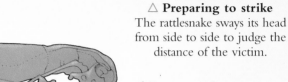

REAR-FANGED   PYTHON OR BOA

ALL SHARP TEETH

Hardly any snakes have blunt teeth for chewing. The teeth are usually slim and sharp, for grabbing prey. In the rear-fanged snakes like the boomslang (*see page 19*), the long fangs are about halfway back in the upper jaw. They have grooves along which the poison flows into the victim. But they cannot swing or tilt, like the front fangs of a viper.

△ **Preparing to strike**
The rattlesnake sways its head from side to side to judge the distance of the victim.

△ **Fangs ready to stab**
The mouth opens slightly so that the long poison fangs can tilt down into position.

◁ **Fearsome fangs**
Rear-fanged snakes usually bite the victim hard and wiggle their jaws so the long poison fangs "saw" into the flesh. Pythons and boas have teeth mainly at the front of the mouth.

SNAKE SKELETON

The snake's skeleton is mostly ribs and backbones. The number of backbones can be more than 400! Some pythons and boas have small rear leg bones. These are left over from long ago, when their ancestors had proper legs. The leg bones form small flaps on the snake's body, but they do not work as legs.

Rear leg bones

△ **Flexible backbone**
Each backbone in the long skeleton can move a little with the backbones in front and behind. This means the snake can curl itself around several times along the whole backbone.

SQUEEZED TO DEATH

Pythons and boas are called constrictors because as they bite their victim, they also wrap their coils around its body and slowly squeeze, or constrict. As the victim breathes out, the snake tightens its grip slightly. The next breath is harder to make, as the snake tightens again. Soon there are no more breaths and the prey is still.

▷ **Boa constrictor**
The common boa (boa constrictor) of America can kill a small prey like a rat in seconds. But it may take 5–10 minutes for a larger victim.

RATTLE, RATTLE

Most snakes give a warning to enemies before they bite in self-defense. Rattlesnakes shake their tail. This has a row of button-shape scales joined together loosely. They make a buzzing or crackling noise as they are "trembled." The diamondback rattlesnake grows up to 7 feet (2 meters) long and is North America's most feared snake.

ANACONDA

TAIPAN

MILK SNAKE

△ **Deadly venom**
The rattlesnake's two long fangs are hollow. Poison flows down through the fangs like an injection from a needle.

△ **Longer rattle, older snake?**
A section is added to the rattle each time the snake moults its skin, twice each year. However, sometimes sections fall off, so rattle length is not a good guide to age.

BEARING BABIES

Most reptiles lay eggs. But some snakes, like boas and sea snakes, give birth to babies. The babies develop inside the mother's body for several months and then emerge through the birth opening. Baby boas are about 20 inches (50 cm) long when born. It takes them ten years or more to grow into adults, when they will be 10 feet (3 meters) or even 13 feet (4 meters) long.

BABY BOAS

COLORED TO HIDE

The colors and patterns of most snakes are for camouflage, to blend in with their surroundings. The anaconda of South America lurks in pools and rivers in the rainforest. The taipan speeds through the dry, scrubby outback of northeast Australia. The milk snake, which is not venomous, has bright colors that make it look like a coral snake, which is poisonous.

CARING FOR THE EGGS

Most snakes lay their eggs in holes or under logs, and leave them to develop and hatch. But several kinds of pythons curl around their eggs and protect them from enemies such as lizards. The Asian python may stay with her eggs for three months. But after they hatch, the mother snake does not look after the babies.

SWALLOWED WHOLE!

The boa crawls forward and around its prey, to engulf it. The jaw bones can move apart so that the mouth becomes wider and higher. Swallowing a big prey might take a half-hour.

The meal is pushed down into the stomach by powerful muscles in the wall of the gullet (food pipe).

△ **Digesting prey**
Once inside the stomach, strong chemicals such as acids begin to eat away at the prey's flesh. The bones, teeth, and other hard parts are usually coughed up later by the boa.

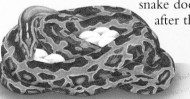

△ **Warming the eggs**
If the weather turns cool, the mother Asian python "shivers" her muscles to make heat. This warms the eggs so they keep developing properly.

LIFE IN A SHELL

The "3 Ts"—turtles, terrapins, and tortoises—have a body part that no other animal possesses. But the "shell" is really two casings, one fixed inside the other, and neither is really a shell! The inner casing is known as the carapace over the top, and the plastron underneath. It is made of about 60 curved bony plates that join firmly together like a glued, box-shaped jigsaw. Attached to this inner "shell" is the outer casing made of large, flat, horny versions of the normal reptile scales, known as scutes. This is what we see on the outside. Most of the "3 Ts" have slow-motion lives, chomping on plant foods or waiting for prey animals to come near.

A GIANT AMONG TORTOISES

Several kinds of giant tortoises are named after their ocean island homes. The Galapagos tortoise of the Pacific has a shell length of more than 3 feet (1 meter) and can weigh well over 440 pounds (200 kg). Almost as huge is the Aldabran tortoise of the Indian Ocean. These peaceful plant-eaters plod to their feeding grounds each morning, then back to their sheltered resting places in the evening. There are about 15,000 of these giants left on the Galapagos, and they need careful conservation.

▽ **Giant tortoise**
Giant tortoises, with their thick shells and great strength, have little to fear. They can live to be well over 100 years old. Some have been taken from their original island homes to other regions as massive "pets."

FLAT AS A PANCAKE!

The pancake tortoise of East Africa is not only very flat, as its name suggests. Its shell is also soft and slightly bendy, because the bony plates and the overlying scutes have slight gaps between them. And this tortoise is no slowpoke—it can run! If danger threatens, it races to shelter and squeezes between rocks or digs quickly into the soil. Like many tortoises, it eats a wide range of plant foods, including grasses, leaves, shoots, and fruits.

NOT SO "COMMON"

The "common" pond turtle of Europe is now quite rare in some places. It has been collected for the pet trade, and its ponds and streams have been polluted or drained away. It basks on a rock or log to warm its body, then dives into the water to hunt small creatures like fish, tadpoles, frogs, and pond insects. But it can also feed on land, on worms, snails, and grubs. So it survives in woods and damp meadows.

◁ **Pancake tortoise**
The pancake tortoise feeds mostly in the morning. In the heat of midday, it crawls into the shade of a low rock or log, so it does not overheat. After its evening meal, it returns to its night "home," a crevice among stones and boulders.

◁ **Handy hinge**
Several turtles and tortoises, like the European pond turtle, have a bendy part or "hinge" near the front of the lower shell. This allows the head to be pulled into the shell more easily for protection.

EXPERT DIGGER

Many tortoises can dig well with their powerful, shovel-shaped front legs. The desert tortoise, of southwest North America, is one of the best diggers. It burrows into the deeper, damper layers of soil to escape the great heat of the desert midday, or the cold night, or a long period of drought. It is medium-sized for a tortoise, with a shell up to 14 inches (35 cm) long.

POPULAR PETS

In the wild, the turtles called pond sliders live from the eastern and southern USA, down to the Amazon region of South America. In captivity, they are bred as pets and live all over the world. They have brightly patterned shells with swirly markings that are different on each turtle—like our fingerprints. Pond sliders prefer to stay in or near water all the time.

◁ **Sharp jaws**
Turtles and tortoises do not have teeth. But they can cut up and chew food with their sharp-edged jaws, which work like curved knife blades. The desert tortoise even chomps on prickly cactus!

Eyes are open for seeing underwater.

Thick leathery skin covers neck and legs.

Unusually long neck.

Wide feet for powerful swimming.

Soft shell.

Long claws for digging prey out of mud.

◁ **Pond sliders**
Young pond sliders eat small water creatures like tadpoles and baby fish. When they grow up, they prefer plants like juicy waterweeds.

REPTILE ROUND-UP

All about chelonians

Turtles, terrapins, and tortoises form the reptile group known as the chelonians.

• There are eight kinds or species of marine turtles, which spend all their lives at sea (*see next page*).
• The tortoises number about 40 species and live in all warmer parts of the world.
• The main turtle group is the emydids, with more than 80 species. They mostly have webbed feet for swimming and include pond sliders, pond turtles, map turtles, box turtles, and terrapins.

UNDERWATER "SNORKEL"

Most turtles spend much of their time in water. Some can stay under a half-hour. But, being reptiles, they must come to the surface to take a breath of air every now and again. The Chinese soft-shelled turtle can breathe while most of its body is still underwater. It stretches its long neck upward and pokes its tubelike nostrils just above the surface. This means that it can stay hidden from land predators for hours at a time.

◁ **Chinese soft-shelled turtle**
The Chinese soft-shelled turtle really does have a soft shell, which feels like thick leather. It is a fierce hunter of many smaller creatures, from water-worms to fish and crayfish.

"FLYING" THROUGH THE SEA

Some turtles hardly ever touch land. Sea turtles spend nearly all their long lives, 60 years or more, cruising through the ocean. Their legs are flippers, with webbed feet for powerful swimming. They surface every few minutes for breaths of air, then dive below the waves to find food. The green sea turtle shown here eats mainly plants. But the biggest of the sea turtles, the massive leatherback, snaps up jellyfish and fish. Every few years, a female sea turtle hauls herself onto the beach, where she herself hatched from an egg, to lay her own.

RACE TO THE SEA

After developing in their eggs, the baby sea turtles hatch and dig to the surface. They are hardly the size of your hand, and must race as fast as possible to the sea. Otherwise they will be caught by predators who gather for a feast. The shells of baby turtles are soft, so seabirds like gulls and skuas can peck through them. Even when the babies reach the water, they can be eaten by fish such as bass and sharks, also octopus and crabs, and even seals and sea-lions. There is danger everywhere!

UP AND DOWN

Sea turtles do not swim by "rowing" their front flippers backward and forward. Instead, they "flap" them up and down. This movement is similar to the way a bird flies through air, and it's also how penguins and seals swim in water. The turtle's rear flippers trail behind the body and help it to steer.

△ **Turtles for dinner**
The tiny turtles waddle as fast as they can toward the water, where they will be safer than on the beach. Seabirds dive onto the baby turtles and snatch them away, perhaps to feed to their own baby chicks.

A sea turtle is strong and streamlined, able to swim as fast as you could jog.

△ **Green turtle**
Grown-up green turtles like plant foods such as sea-grass, and the roots of mangrove trees that grow along tropical coasts.

GREENS FOR THE GREEN

The green turtle grows to a large size, with a shell up to 47 inches (120 cm) long. It may weigh 660 pounds (300 kg)—as much as four people. When young, it eats animal food such as sea-snails and baby shellfish. But as it grows up, it becomes more of a vegetarian.

Powerful muscles in the turtle's shoulders pull up the front flippers and twist them slightly toward the top of the shell.

The turtle's chest muscles make the front flippers sweep downward and push backward against the water.

LONG-DISTANCE WANDERERS

Most sea turtles wander huge distances across the oceans. Some can cover more than 1,800 miles (3,000 km) in one year. We know this because scientists have fixed small radio-beacons, like cell phones, to their shells. The beacon sends out radio signals that are tracked by satellites.

◁ **Home again**

After a few years of wandering, most turtles return to the area where they hatched as babies. The females and males mate, then the females come ashore to lay eggs.

Fertile female ▷

Over a few weeks, the female green turtle lays six or seven batches of eggs in different holes, making more than 1,000 eggs altogether.

DIGGING IN THE DARK

A female green turtle drags herself up the beach under cover of dark. She digs a deep hole in the sand and lays about 100–150 eggs in the bottom. Then she fills in the hole and smooths over the sand, so that egg-stealing predators like foxes, otters, gulls, lizards, and crabs cannot find it. Finally, after a couple of hours of tremendous effort, she hauls herself back into the sea.

INSIDE THE SHELL

A turtle's insides are packed within the shell for protection. Like all reptiles, it breathes air using lungs. But the turtle cannot make its chest bigger and smaller when breathing, like other animals, because the shell is too stiff. So as the lungs fill up with air, the guts and muscles are pushed backward. The lungs are in the upper part of the shell, filled with air like a balloon. This helps the turtle to float and stay the right way up.

The powerful swimming muscles are fixed to the leg bones at one end, and the shoulder and hip bones at the other end.

Lungs

Stomach

Spleen

Small intestines

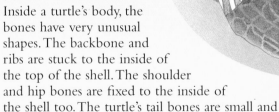

SHELL AND BONES

Inside a turtle's body, the bones have very unusual shapes. The backbone and ribs are stuck to the inside of the top of the shell. The shoulder and hip bones are fixed to the inside of the shell too. The turtle's tail bones are small and short, but the skull inside the head is very big, with a boxlike shape.

Webbed toe bones make a wide surface for pushing the water.

TURTLES GREAT AND SMALL

The snapping turtle of North and Central America is probably the fiercest and could easily bite off your finger. It grows to about 20 inches (50 cm) long. Sometimes it lies almost buried in the mud, with only eyes and nostrils showing.

The matamata of South America lies on the bottom of swamps and rivers, waiting for prey to come near. Its frilly head and spiky shell make it look like bits of old leaves, twigs, and stones on the riverbed.

Biggest of all turtles is the leatherback— 7 feet (2 meters) long and more than 1,100 pounds (500 kg) in weight. It lives all its life at sea and can dive down more than 330 feet (100 meters) for over 20 minutes.

Terrapins can live on water and land. They bask in the sun to get warm, but if danger comes near, they quickly dive into the water and swim away fast.

SNAPPER

MATAMATA

LEATHERBACK

TERRAPIN

LEARNING ABOUT REPTILES

Long ago, people knew about reptiles. In Australia, drawings over 20,000 years old on rocks and caves show crocodiles and turtles. The people who made the pictures probably ate the turtles, and feared being eaten by the crocs! More than 3,000 years ago, people in Ancient Egypt kept Nile crocodiles in tanks and preserved their bodies as mummies. Today we know huge amounts about all kinds of reptiles—but there is plenty more to find out. One vital reason for learning about them is to save them. Many kinds of reptiles have become very rare, and some are in danger of extinction—dying out forever. These reptiles need our help now!

▽ **Reptile "cows"**
American alligators are bred and raised in much the same way as cows and sheep on ordinary farms. The world center for 'gator farming is Louisiana, and the trade is worth more than $50 million each year.

NOT THEIR FAULT
We can't really blame poisonous snakes for biting people. The snakes are usually just defending themselves. As we chop down forests, plow up grasslands, and drain marshes to use the land for our own needs, snakes and reptiles of all kinds have fewer places to live. This problem, known as habitat loss, is the single biggest threat to all kinds of wildlife around the world.

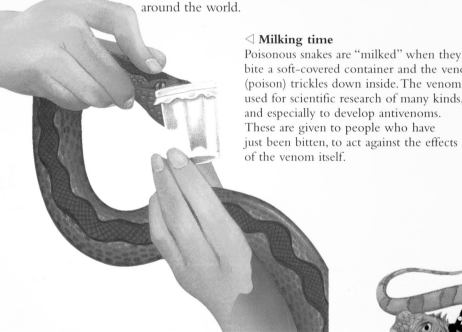

◁ **Milking time**
Poisonous snakes are "milked" when they bite a soft-covered container and the venom (poison) trickles down inside. The venom is used for scientific research of many kinds, and especially to develop antivenoms. These are given to people who have just been bitten, to act against the effects of the venom itself.

DOWN ON THE 'GATOR FARM
In 1967, the American alligator was listed as an endangered species. Hunting it became illegal. Some 'gators were captured and raised in ponds on "farms." This provided a supply of meat for people and pets to eat, and skins or hides to make into belts, bags, shoes, and similar items—meat and hides that would otherwise come from wild alligators. Eggs and babies from the captive 'gators were then put back into the wild. The result was that this species was taken off the endangered list in 1987.

A GROWING PROBLEM
Reptiles like lizards, snakes, turtles, and tortoises make popular pets. But some owners do not think ahead. Many snakes need regular supplies of living prey, which the owners must obtain. Some turtles and tortoises live naturally in tropical regions, but become pets in cooler places, where they soon fall ill. Crocodiles seem almost "cute" when babies. But as they grow, they become more difficult to feed and contain. Planning to keep any pet requires great thought and care—especially so for reptiles.

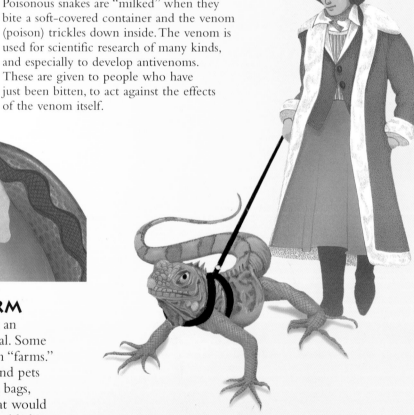

△ **A demanding pet**
A lizard like a green iguana can grow to 7 feet (2 meters) long, and it has powerful muscles and sharp claws. A pet like this can become a real handful!

◁ **Snake snacks**
"Do you serve snakes here?"
In places such as China,
snakes are just another type
of meat for the dinner table.

▽ **Round Island boa**
The Round Island boa lives only on a tiny
island in the Indian Ocean. It is one of the
world's rarest reptiles, with probably 500 or
fewer left. Experts are trying to save the
species by breeding these boas in captivity.

TASTY TREAT

Many reptiles end up as food for people. Is this a
problem? In regions of the world such as East Asia,
snake and turtle and alligator meat have been eaten in
traditional meals for centuries. The meat itself can be
tasty and nutritious. Reptile eggs are also eaten. But
capturing reptiles from the wild means their numbers
have dwindled. Also the reptiles are sometimes kept in
terrible conditions before being killed and eaten.

WATCH OUT, SNAKES ABOUT

There are many poisonous snakes. But only a few
species kill people on a regular basis. They include the
black mamba, Russell's viper, common krait, Indian
cobra, and taipan. Most of these snakes are dangerous
only if they are surprised or cornered. Also they usually
give a warning before they strike—for example, by
rearing up and hissing. Sometimes bites happen because
people ignore basic safety, like not putting their hands
into holes, and not walking around barefoot.

▷ **Warning! Avoid me!**
Some snakes are black with yellow or red
patterns, like the banded krait of South Asia.
These color patterns are often used on our
warning signs. Snakes have them
for the same reason. The banded
krait's venom is 15 times more
powerful than the cobra's.

ALMOST GONE

Conservation experts describe a species
of animal as "critically endangered" when it is so rare and
threatened that it could die out in 10–20 years. More than
60 species of reptiles fall into this group. Some live only
on tiny islands, where their eggs and young are eaten by
introduced predators—cats, rats, stoats, foxes, and other
predators brought to the islands by people. Others, like
sea turtles, have their egg-laying places disturbed.

TURTLE SHELL

STOP THE REPTILE TRADE

CITES is the Convention on
International Trade in
Endangered Species. This
worldwide agreement bans
selling or trade of many
reptiles and other animals
(and plants, too). It includes
not only live animals, but also
their body parts and products,
such as turtle shells, snake skins,
and crocodile teeth. But trade
continues in some areas—often because
thoughtless people from
rich countries have
enough money to
buy these products.

CROCODILE TEETH

GLOSSARY AND INDEX

backbones Individual bones, known as vertebrae, which form a row or chain in the spinal column of a reptile—*see* vertebrates.

camouflage When a living thing is colored and patterned to resemble or merge into its surroundings so that it is less noticeable.

carnivore A creature that eats mainly other animals, including their meat, flesh, and other body parts.

chelonians The scientific name for the reptile group which includes turtles, terrapins, and tortoises.

cold-blooded An animal that cannot make its own heat to keep its body warm. Reptiles are cold-blooded, while birds and mammals are warm-blooded (*see below*).

colubrids Poisonous snakes which have their long fangs toward the rear of the mouth, such as the boomslang.

conservation Saving or preserving animals and plants so that they do not become extinct (die out forever). The best long-term way to do this is by protecting natural places or habitats with all their wildlife.

constrictors Types of snakes that coil around and squeeze or constrict their prey. The best-known kinds are pythons and boas.

crocodilians The scientific name for the reptile group which includes crocodiles, alligators, caimans, and gharials.

dragon Among reptiles, several kinds of large lizards are known as dragons, like the Komodo dragon. Different kinds of "dragons" with scales and wings and fiery breath are featured in make-believe legends and fairy-tales, but do not really exist.

elapids Poisonous snakes which have their long fangs at the front of the mouth, such as the cobras, mambas, and kraits.

fang A long, slim, sharp tooth, especially one which can release poison (venom).

gape To open the mouth wide, as when snakes bite their prey, or crocodiles lie open-mouthed to lose heat and cool their bodies.

habitat A type of place or surrounding, to which an animal is suited or adapted, such as a pond, wood, desert, or seashore.

Mesozoic Era The time period from about 250 million to 65 million years ago, when dinosaurs and other reptiles ruled the land, sea, and air. It is often called the "Age of Reptiles."

pit (pit organ) In some snakes, a bowl-like hole below the eye. It can detect the heat given off by close objects, including warm-blooded prey like birds and mammals.

predator An animal that hunts or pursues other creatures, known as its prey.

prey A creature that is hunted by another animal, known as the predator.

ribs Long, slim bones around the front of the chest. In some reptiles, ribs are extra-long and can be moved or tilted to hold out flaps of skin.

scales The body covering of most reptiles, scales are usually small, hard, and flattened, and give protection as well as colors and patterns.

scutes Larger, stronger, bonier versions of the normal reptile scales, covering reptiles such as turtles and crocodiles.

species A main kind of living thing. Individuals in a species look similar and can breed with each other, but not with members of other species.

squamates The scientific name for the reptile group which includes the snakes and the lizards (even legless lizards like slow-worms).

strike In snakes and similar animals, to bite very quickly with a quick lunge forward.

venom A poisonous substance secreted by venomous or poisonous snakes.

vertebrates Creatures with a backbone or spinal column of bones (vertebrae) along the middle of the body. They include fish, amphibians, reptiles, birds, and mammals.

warm-blooded An animal that can make its own heat to keep its body warm. The two main groups of warm-blooded animals are birds and mammals, while reptiles are cold-blooded.